THE COMMUNITY OF OUR MILITARY BASE

Portia Summers

Enslow Publishing
101 W. 23rd Street
Suite 240
New York, NY 10011
USA

enslow.com

WORDS TO KNOW

civilian—A person who is not in the military.

commissary—The grocery store for people who live on a base.

deployed—Sent away from home for military duty.

hangar—A large covered area where aircraft are stored and repaired.

immediate family—A person's close family members.

military base—An area that houses soldiers and their families, as well as military equipment and technology.

PX (post exchange)—The department store for people who live on the base.

rank—A soldier's position in the military.

stationed—Sent somewhere to do a military job.

veterans—Retired soldiers from the military.

CONTENTS

A military base community is made up of soldiers, their families, and many others who work on the base.

A Military Community

A community is a group of people who live and work together. Communities can be found everywhere. Some are in cities. Some are in the country. And some communities can be found on military bases.

A military base is an area, provided by the Army, Navy, Air Force, Coast Guard, or Marines, where soldiers and their families live and work. Military bases can be found all over the world, from Alaska to Zimbabwe.

Soldiers of every rank, religion, and gender live on military bases. Many of them have families. Immediate family members are allowed to live on the military bases with them.

A Community of Support

The military base provides housing, hospitals, schools, and even grocery stores for the people who live there. When soldiers are deployed, or sent away on duty, their families wait for their safe return on the military base, often with other families waiting for soldiers to return. Military bases offer not only a place for soldiers and their families to live, but also support for the people who live there.

Often military bases will have fun activities for families, like this field day.

Who Lives on a Military Base?

A military base supports soldiers and their families. Children, husbands, wives, teachers, doctors, and soldiers all live there. Many military bases also provide houses for veterans, or retired soldiers.

Every military base also has schools and day care for the children who live there. Many teachers spend a lot of time on military bases.

A Marine helps children cross the street on their way to school on the military base.

Hospitals and Law Enforcement

Military bases also have hospitals, which need staff like doctors and nurses. Many of the doctors and nurses are in the military, but some are not. All are welcome on the military base.

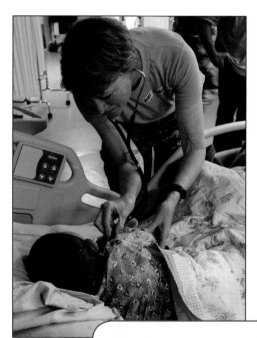

Many military bases help with local law enforcement, so sometimes civilian police work on a military base. They do not live there, but many often work with the soldiers and their families there.

An Army nurse checks on a young patient at the base hospital.

Largest Military Base in the United States

The largest army base in the United States is Fort Bragg in North Carolina. About 238,650 people live on the 163,000-acre base. There are active duty soldiers as well as reserves and military students, civilian employees, veterans, and their family members all living together on the base.

Fort Bragg

11

What's on a Military Base?

A military base provides housing for soldiers and their families. Depending on the size of the family, they may be given an apartment or a house. Houses could be big or small, and they may be built in a special way depending on where they are. For example, houses on military bases in Alaska are built to keep out the cold. They have special shades to block out the sun during the time of the year when the sun never sets.

Military bases in hot, desert areas such as Arizona have powerful air conditioners and special roofs that keep the sun from overheating the home.

A lot of military housing looks just like houses you would see in an ordinary neighborhood.

Military bases also provide community centers where families can take classes, and children can go to special camps during the summer.

Every military base also has a gym and a pool, as well as places for families to rent equipment such as RVs, boats, four-wheelers, cars, and anything else needed for a fun vacation or Saturday off.

On every military base is a post exchange, or PX. This is similar to a department store. Prices here are cheaper than stores off base, and families can shop for clothes, electronics, household items, and other things they might need. A commissary is also on every military base. Like the PX, the prices here are cheaper than stores off-base, but a commissary sells groceries instead of household items.

A member of the Air Force buys groceries at the commissary.

Overseas Military Bases

When soldiers are sent overseas, many times their families can go with them. Overseas military bases provide extra goods and services that the bases in the United States don't provide. Veterinarians live on base to take care of family pets. A furniture store is also on overseas bases, so that families can furnish their new homes. Only bases in Alaska and Hawaii in the United States provide these services. On the other military bases around the United States, families have to leave the base for these services.

Each military base provides schools for the children that live there. Day cares, elementary schools, middle schools, and high schools are all on military bases, filled with students whose parents are in the military. Since many families are often moved around as their soldiers are stationed in different locations, it is comforting to be in school with other students who have to move frequently.

17

An Air Force pilot reads to children at a base preschool.

Military bases also have hospitals, where soldiers and their families can get health care. Many babies are born in military hospitals and receive care from doctors in military hospitals their whole lives.

A military obstacle course

Military Training

Of course, military bases must have places for soldiers to train and work. There are buildings for technology, training, and education. Airplanes, helicopters, and hangars are often found on military bases, complete with runways and mechanic shops. There are special obstacle courses where soldiers can train, as well as classrooms for them to learn new military methods.

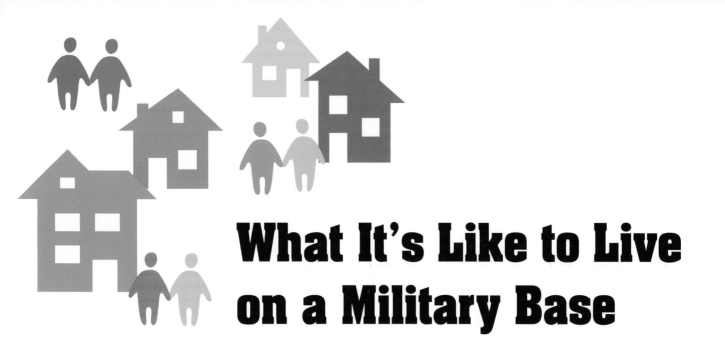

What It's Like to Live on a Military Base

Living on a military base can be fun. Not only are you living near people who understand what it is like to live in a military family, but you also have many things provided for you.

Many military bases have community parties, barbecues, and dances, as well as events such as concerts, plays, and movie nights.

Families on a military base get together to enjoy food and friends.

Living on a military base provides a safe, welcome community for soldiers and their families. The government provides these homes for the soldiers who live their lives protecting the freedom of the people of the United States. Soldiers can do their jobs better knowing that their families are taken care of. Military bases provide much more than housing for families. They create a special community just for them.

ACTIVITY: YOU AND THE MILITARY BASE COMMUNITY

1. There are many children your age who live on military bases across the country and around the world. Using what you have learned so far, imagine what it would be like to live in a military base community as a young person.

2. Brainstorm some ideas about how your life would be different on a military base compared to your own community, whether it is a city, suburb, or farming community. What are some things that might be the same? (If you do live on a military base, compare your community to a different one.)

3. On a blank sheet of paper, copy down the Venn diagram shown on page 23. Label one circle "My Community" and the other "Military Base Community." In the overlapping area in the middle, write down things that would be similar (such as subjects studied in school and spending time with friends).

4. On the outer edges of the two circles, write down how the two communities would differ (people you would meet, concerns about family members, friendships, places you would go, etc.).

5. Look at your completed diagram. Did you find more similarities or differences between the two communities? Do you think you would enjoy living in a military base community?

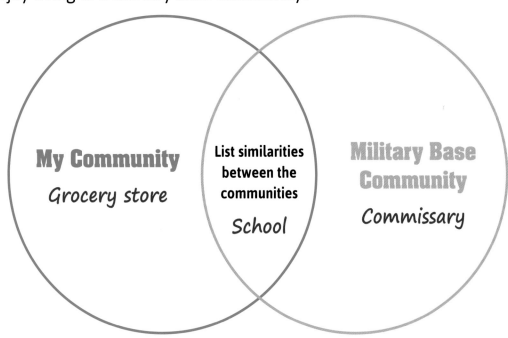

My Community

Grocery store

List similarities between the communities

School

Military Base Community

Commissary

LEARN MORE

Books

Harrington, Claudia. *My Military Mom.* Edina, MN: Looking Glass Library, 2015.

Kohl, Peter. *My Dad Is in the Army.* New York: PowerKids Press, 2016.

Sicilian, Devin, and Victor Juhaz. *H is for Honor: A Military Family Alphabet.* Ann Arbor, MI: Sleeping Bear Press, 2014.

Websites

PBS Kids
pbskids.org/rogers/buildANeighborhood.html
Build your own neighborhood!

Military Kids Connect
militarykidsconnect.dcoe.mil/kids
Play games, create projects, and more.

INDEX

Published in 2017 by Enslow Publishing, LLC.
101 W. 23rd Street, Suite 240, New York, NY 10011
Copyright © 2017 by Enslow Publishing, LLC
All rights reserved.

No part of this book may be reproduced by any means without the written permission of the publisher.

Library of Congress Cataloging-in-Publication Data
Names: Summers, Portia, author.
Title: The community of our military base / Portia Summers.
Description: New York, NY : Enslow Publishing, [2017] | Series: Zoom in on communities | Includes bibliographical references and index. | Audience: Grades K-3.
Identifiers: LCCN 2015045448| ISBN 9780766078130 (library bound) | ISBN 9780766078116 (pbk.) | ISBN 9780766078123 (6-pack)
Subjects: LCSH: Military bases--United States--Juvenile literature.
Classification: LCC UC403 .S86 2016 | DDC 355.1/2920973--dc23
LC record available at http://lccn.loc.gov/2015045448

Printed in Malaysia

To Our Readers: We have done our best to make sure all website addresses in this book were active and appropriate when we went to press. However, the author and the publisher have no control over and assume no liability for the material available on those websites or on any websites they may link to. Any comments or suggestions can be sent by e-mail to customerservice@enslow.com.

Photo Credits: Cover, p. 1 Education Images/UIG via Getty Images; graphics throughout Kev Draws/Shutterstock.com (people circle), antoshkaforever/Shutterstock.com (people holding hands), 3d_kot/Shutterstock.com (houses); p. 4 Kim Karpeles/Alamy Stock Photo; p. 7 US Air Force photo by Airman 1st Class Luke J Kitterman; p. 9 LUKE FRAZZA/AFP/Getty Images; p. 10 615 collection/Alamy Stock Photo; p. 11 Jonas N. Jordan, U.S. Army Corps of Engineers/File:Fort Bragg 1st Brigade barracks.jpg/Wikimedia Commons; p. 13 Patti McConville/Alamy Stock Photo; p. 15 Joe Amon/The Denver Post via Getty Images; p. 17 Airman 1st Class Zachary Hada; p. 18; US Army photo By Staff Sgt Christopher Bergman; p. 20 US Marine Corps Photo by Sgt Christopher Q Stone 26th MEU Combat Camera; p. 21 Blend Images/Alamy Stock Photo.